wild, w

SHARKS

AND OTHER DANGEROUS FISH

Written by
Denny Robson
Illustrated by
James Field

This is a Parragon Publishing Book
This edition printed for Books Are Fun in 2001

Parragon Publishing
Queen Street House
4 Queen Street
Bath BA1 1HE, UK

Produced by

David West Children's Books
7 Princeton Court
55 Felsham Road
Putney
London SW15 1AZ, UK

British Library Cataloguing-in-Publication Data

A catalogue record for this book is available from the British Library.

Hardback: ISBN 0-75254-686-4
Paperback: ISBN 0-75255-621-5

Printed in Italy

Designers
Jenny Skelly
Aarti Parmar
Illustrator
James Field
(SGA)
Rob Shone
Cartoonist
Peter Wilks
(SGA)
Editor
James Pickering
Consultant
Steve Parker

CONTENTS

What are sharks?

Sharks are meat-eating sea fish. Most have sleek bodies and rows of sharp teeth. There are about 375 types, of different shapes and sizes, living in different parts of the world. The dwarf shark is only four inches long, while the whale shark, the biggest of all fish, is nearly 50 feet.

How old are sharks?

Fossils show that sharks appeared more than 350 million years ago, long before the dinosaurs. Megalodon was a huge shark which hunted large prey and probably ate shellfish too. Its teeth were over three inches long.

Amazing! Sharks become sluggish in cool water, and so most prefer to live in warm seas. But the huge Greenland shark, 20 feet long, enjoys icy water. It lives in the North Atlantic, hunting for fish and seals beneath the pack ice.

Is it true?
All sharks are dangerous.

No. In the order of dangerous sharks, the great white is most feared by people. But most sharks are harmless to us, and will only attack if they are disturbed. Other dangerous sharks include the tiger shark, mako, bronze and black-tipped whalers, and hammerhead.

Are sharks different from other fish?

Sharks, and their relatives the skates and rays, have skeletons made of rubbery cartilage. Other fish have skeletons made of bone. A shark's gill slits are not covered like other fish, but are in a row behind its head.

How fast can a shark swim?

Sharks such as the mako shark are perfect swimming machines, capable of speeds of up to 45 mph. Their sleek shape means they can move and turn quickly through the water.

Is it true?
Sharks never have a break.

No. Sharks living near the surface must swim all their lives to avoid sinking. But others like the nurse shark spend most of their time motionless on the seabed. Nurse sharks can pump water over their gills and so they don't need to keep moving.

Gray reef shark

Why are sharks darker on top?

Sharks which swim near the surface are dark on top and paler on their undersides. This means they are difficult to see from above or below as they hunt for prey.

Amazing! Most sharks drown if they stop swimming, as no oxygen-rich water is passing over their gills. They also sink. They do not have a swim bladder like other fish. They have a huge oily liver instead, which helps to keep them afloat.

How do sharks breathe?

Like all fish, sharks extract oxygen from the water using their gills. Water enters their mouths, and oxygen is absorbed as the water passes over the red, feathery, blood-filled gills. Most sharks keep moving all the time in order to get a constant supply of oxygen.

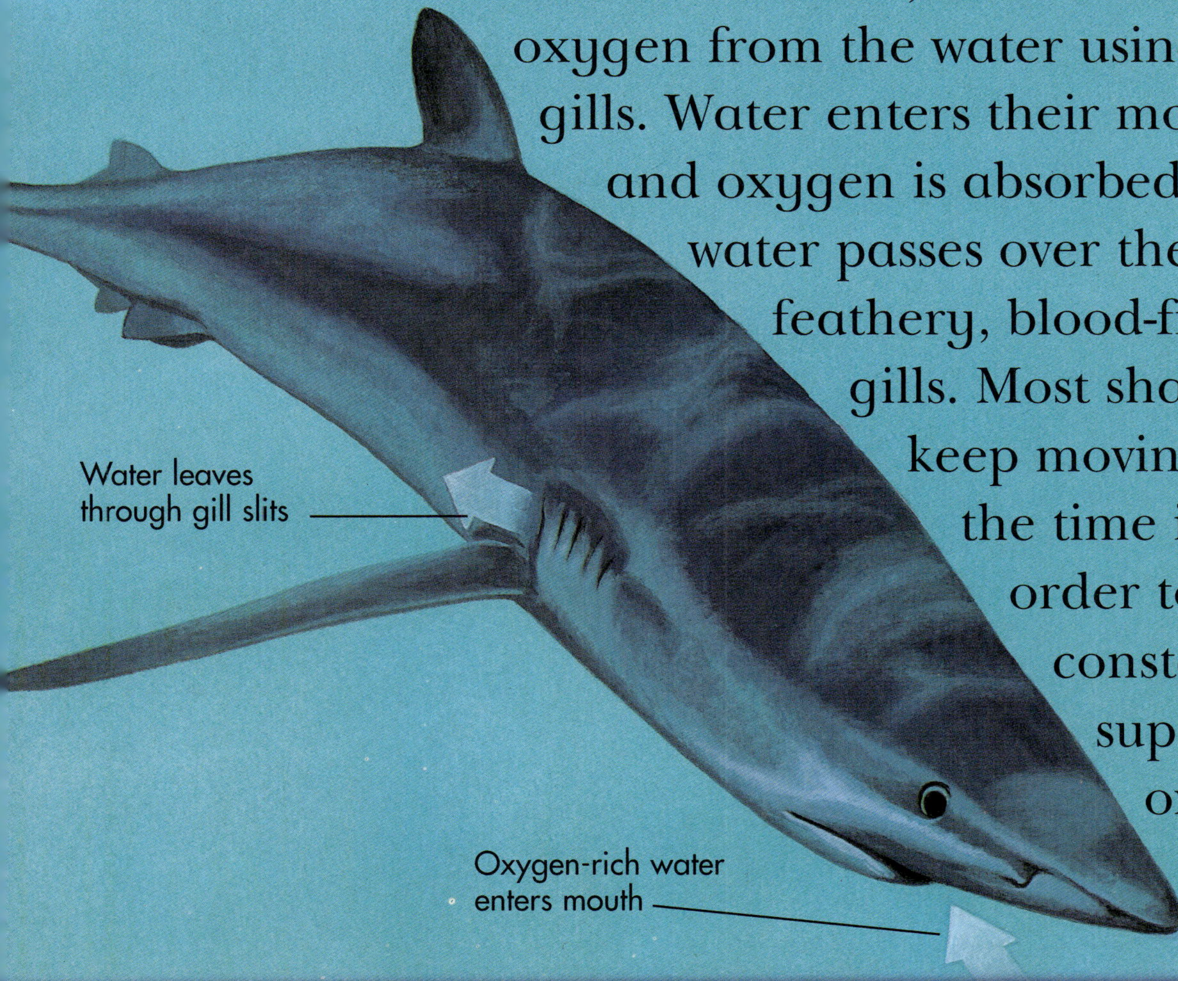

Sand tiger shark

Do sharks have the same senses as us?

Sharks have the five senses of sight, smell, taste, hearing and touch. They also have one more. Sensitive cells on their snouts allow them to pick up tiny electrical signals from other animals.

Reef sharks

How do sharks know when an animal is struggling nearby?

Sharks can tell that there are animals in their area, even when there is no blood to smell. A sensitive 'lateral line' along their bodies allows them to feel ripples in the water from any struggling animal or person.

Do sharks have good eyesight?

Sight is important in the final moments of a shark's hunt. But sharks depend much more on their sense of smell. Sharks get very excited at the smell of blood. They can smell a drop of blood, diluted millions of times, half a mile away.

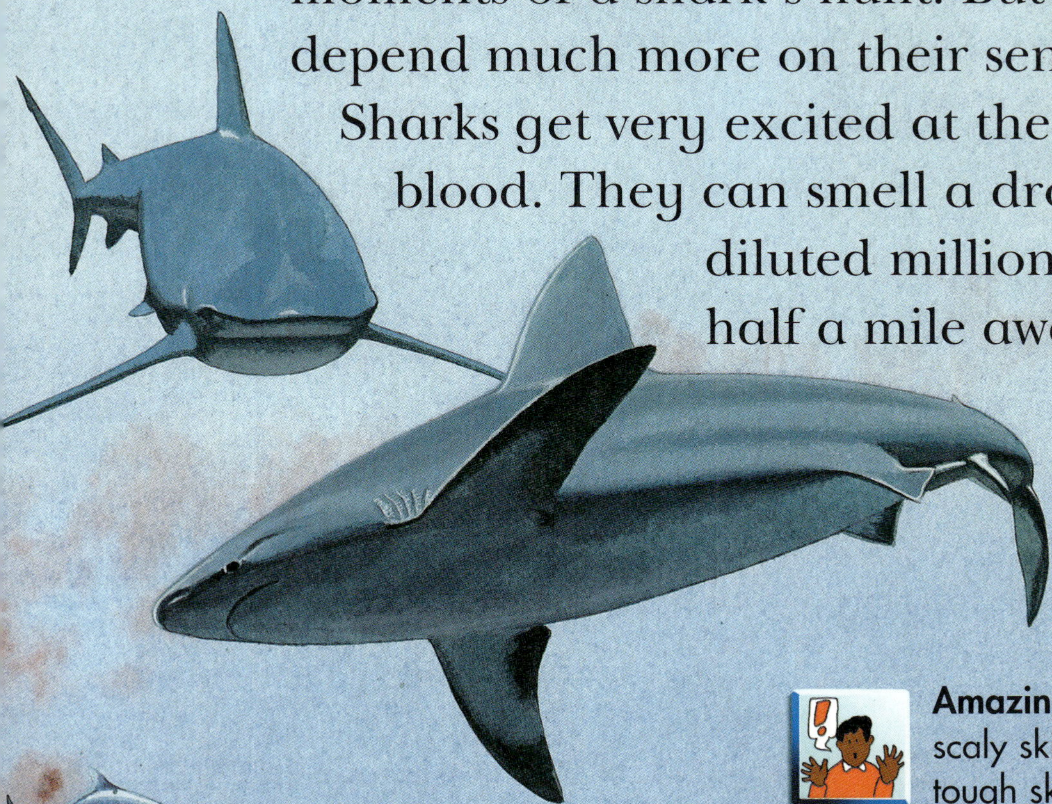

Amazing! Most fish have scaly skin, but a shark's tough skin and scales are very different. They are sharp points called denticles which are like teeth. Shark skin was once used for smoothing down wood, instead of sandpaper.

Is it true?
Sharks nudge their food before they take a bite.

Yes. They sometimes nudge an object or animal with their snout before they decide whether to eat it or not! Perhaps they can "taste" it with special cells in their skin.

Denticles

What eats its unborn brothers and sisters?

With some sharks only a few baby sharks, or pups, are born. This is because the first pups to develop eat the other eggs and embryos inside the mother. Often only one mako pup survives because it eats all the others.

Adult and young mako

Amazing! Some sharks take nine months to develop inside the mother, as long as a human baby. But the spiny dogfish takes 24 months! Young sharks are then on their own, even though it may be years before they are ready for the open sea.

Do sharks lay eggs?

In most sharks, fertilized eggs develop inside the female's body. But some sharks lay eggs and then swim away, leaving the eggs to develop on their own. Dogfish lay eggs in leathery cases, which are called "mermaid's purses".

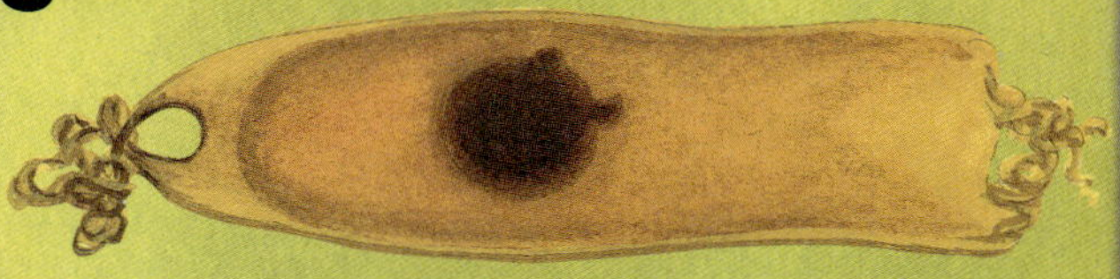

Swell shark embryo at one-month-old

Three-month-old embryo

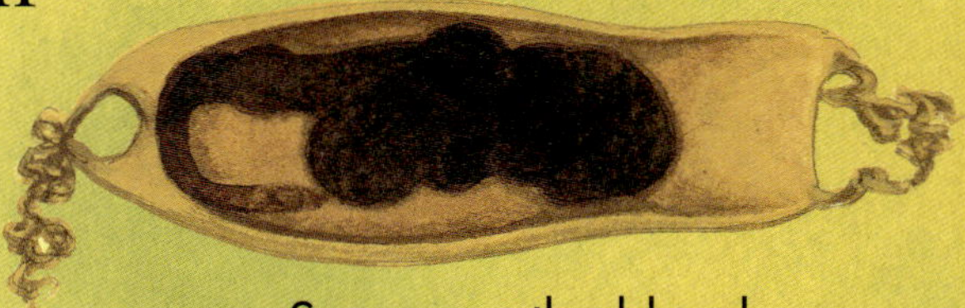

Seven-month-old embryo

Is it true?
Sharks never eat their own young.

No. Some sharks give birth, and then if they come across their pup later in the day they will eat it!

Hammerhead shark pups

What gives birth to lots of pups?

As many as 40 hammerhead shark pups may be born in one litter. They develop in a similar way to human babies, inside their mother's body.

What is known as the trash can of the sea?

Tiger sharks will eat anything. They are not put off by a crunchy turtle shell, or a stinging jellyfish, or even a poisonous snake. They will happily munch dead animals that have been washed out to sea, old boots, papers, tin cans, plastic bags – and even people!

Amazing! Sometimes when a shark feeds, others join in. They get excited at the blood and movement around them, and seem to go crazy, biting, twisting and turning wildly in a "feeding frenzy".

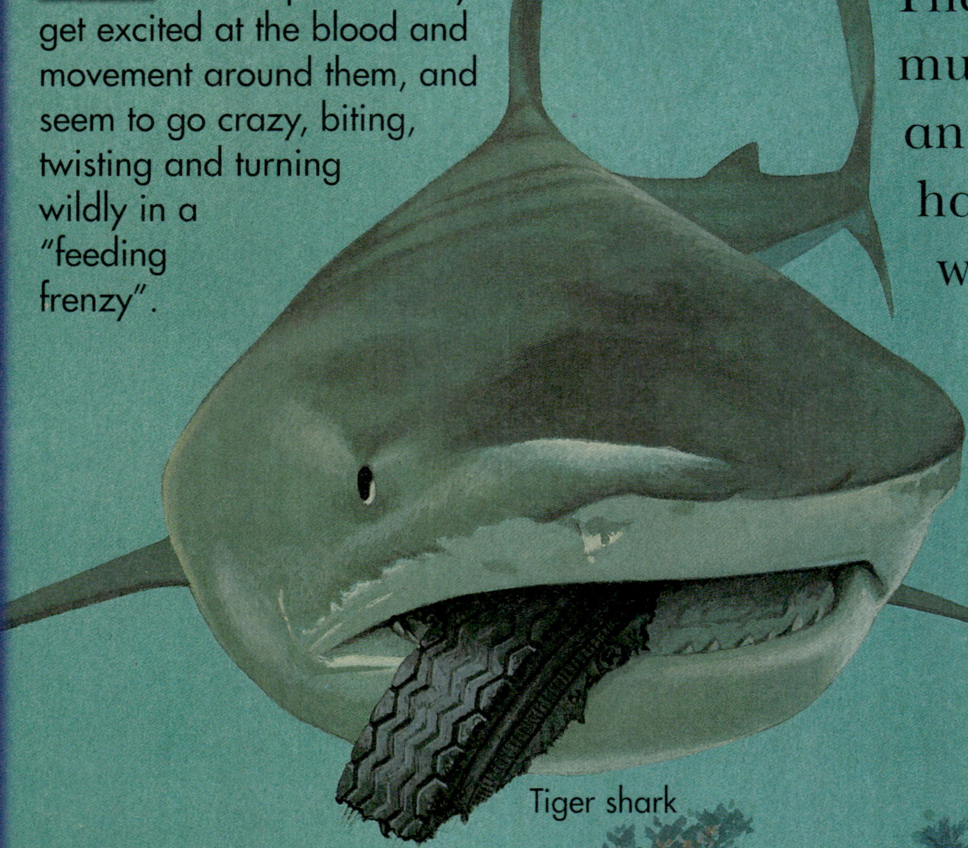

Tiger shark

Sand tiger shark

How many teeth do sharks have?

Sharks are born with jaws full of teeth, neatly arranged in rows. They grow teeth all their lives. When front ones wear out or are lost, they're replaced by new teeth behind.

Is it true?
A shark's teeth last for months.

No. Once a rear tooth has moved to the front row, it may drop out, snap off or be worn away in as little as two weeks.

Do all sharks have the same teeth?

The shape and size depend on a shark's food. For example, the great white has slicing teeth for tearing off chunks of seal or dolphin. The Port Jackson has sharp front teeth to hold shellfish, and blunt back teeth to crush them.

Tiger shark tooth

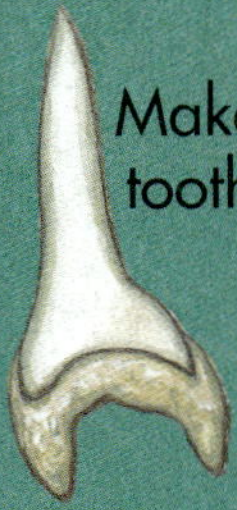

Mako tooth

Great white shark tooth

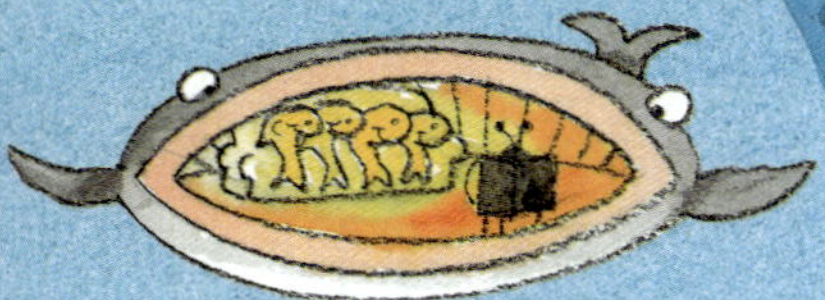

Amazing! It's almost impossible for sharks to get rid of parasites. Tiny creatures eat parasite eggs, fish eat the tiny creatures, and then sharks eat the fish!

Is it true?
Remora fish will feed inside a shark's mouth.

Yes. A whale shark is so big that there's lots of space for remoras. Some attach themselves to the whale shark's mouth and will even swim inside the mouth and gills to find food.

Lemon shark with remoras

Pilot fish

What uses a sucker to hitch a ride?

Remoras are strange fish with large suction pads on the top of their heads. They use these to cling on to sharks. When they peel off to steal scraps, they must take care that the shark doesn't eat them.

Which travelers harm sharks?

Tiny creatures called parasites feed on a shark's skin, inside its guts and in its blood. Some even settle and feed on the surface of its eye, making it difficult for the shark to see.

Parasites feeding on a shark's fin

What hides in a shark's shadow?

Just like remoras, pilot fish also travel with sharks. They're quick and agile as they swim alongside the shark. They hide in the shark's shadow, safe from their enemies, and dart out to snap up any leftovers from the latest kill.

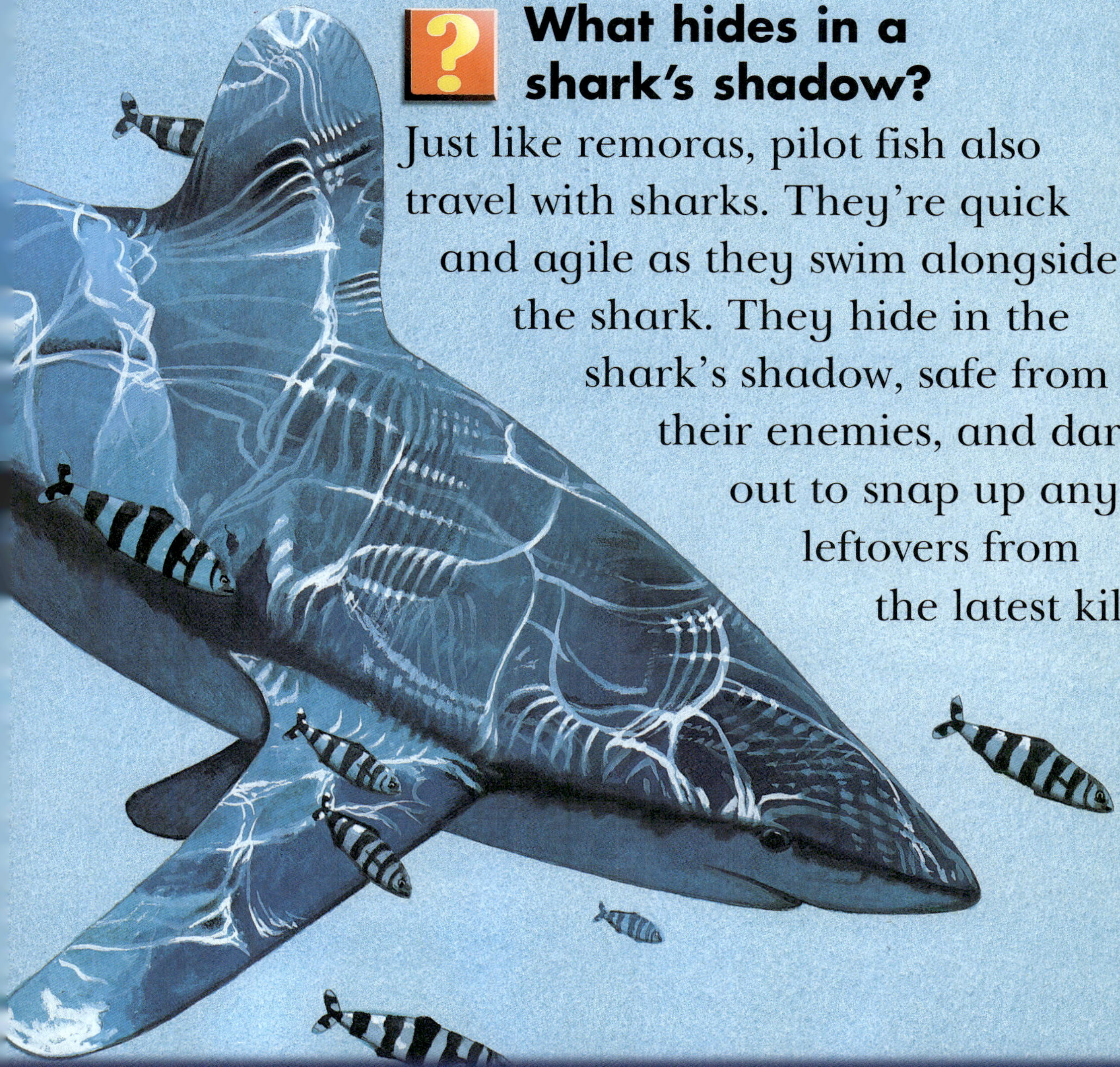

What can attack with its tail?

The thresher shark has a long and powerful tail, often longer than its main body, which it uses like a whip. Like dolphins, thresher sharks hunt in packs. They use their tails to stun fish or to round them up ready for attack.

Thresher sharks

Seal

Mako shark

Which is the fastest shark of all?

The mako shark can move through water as quickly as 45 mph. If an angler catches one, it sometimes leaps out of the water into the air as it tries to escape.

What can swallow a seal whole?

The great white shark, also known as "white death", is a powerful predator which often swallows its prey whole. Luckily, it thinks that seals and sea lions are much tastier than human beings!

Amazing! Bull sharks are unusual because they prefer shark meat to other flesh. They're one of few sharks to spend time in fresh water. They swim up rivers and can enter lakes.

Is it true?
Sharks have to eat every day.

No. After a good kill, a great white shark could last three months without food before it needs to eat again.

What is the biggest fish in the world?

The biggest fish is also one of the most harmless, the whale shark. It measures 50 feet long and weighs about 13 tons. It swims slowly through the sea with its mouth open wide, filtering millions of tiny creatures from the water.

Is it true?
You could hitch a ride on a whale shark.

Yes. These gentle giants have been known to allow scuba divers to hang on to their fins and ride with them.

Amazing! Little is known about the megamouth. But we do know that it has luminous organs that give off a glow around its lips. Scientists think this may be to tempt tiny creatures into its mouth.

Basking shark

Which shark appears to sunbathe?

Basking sharks spend much of their time wallowing at the ocean's surface, especially when it's sunny – probably because there's more food there on sunny days, not because they want a suntan!

What has a huge mouth?

The megamouth shark lives in deep, dark seas. Like the whale shark, it swims with its enormous mouth wide open, filtering water for food. It is very rare and only a few have ever been seen.

Megamouth

Which shark has wings?

Angel sharks have very large pectoral fins, like an angel's wings. They spend much of their lives on the ocean floor, waiting for fish or shellfish to come along so they can snap them up.

Angel shark

Is it true?
Angel sharks look like monks.

Yes. Angel sharks are also called monkfish because their heads are the same shape as a monk's hood.

Port Jackson shark

What is a "pig fish"?

The Port Jackson shark is known as the "pig fish", or "bulldog shark". It has a blunt head and a squashed nose with very large nostrils for finding sea urchins and shellfish.

Which shark uses a disguise?

The wobbegong shark is a master of disguise. The coloring and markings of its flattened body help it blend into its surroundings on the seabed. It also has a "beard" of skin around its mouth which looks just like seaweed to unsuspecting prey.

Amazing! If a swell shark is attacked by a predator, it gulps down as much sea water as it can, and swells up like a balloon. It then jams itself into a crack in a rock where its enemy can't reach it.

Which mysterious shark has a very long snout?

Goblin sharks were discovered 100 years ago and yet we still know very little about them. They live in deep water, and use their long, sensitive snouts to seek out prey.

What has a head like a hammer?

The head of a hammerhead shark is spread out to form a T-shape with its body. Its eyes are on each end of the "hammer". As it swims, it swings its head from side to side so it can look around.

Is it true?
Cookiecutter sharks can glow.

Yes. These small sharks have light organs on their undersides, which glow, maybe to persuade their prey to come close to them.

What bites chunks out of its prey?

Cookiecutter sharks are often happy with just a bite or two from their prey, which includes whales, seals and dolphins. The wounds they make with their small teeth are oval-shaped, a bit like a cookie.

Seal wounded by cookiecutter

Amazing! Hammerhead sharks have few enemies and they feed alone. Yet they sometimes gather together in large "schools", where hundreds all swim together.

Is it true?
A sawfish has "teeth" on its snout.

Yes. Sawfish and saw sharks have long sharp snouts studded with teeth, like a saw. They use their snouts to dig in the mud for food and to slash at other fish. The six types of sawfish belong to the same group as rays.

What is called the devilfish?

Manta rays are also known as devilfish, even though they are harmless and feed on plankton. They are the largest of all rays, at 23 feet across. They flap their huge fins like wings, which makes them look as if they're flying slowly and gracefully through the water.

Electric ray

Amazing! Rays and skates may look very different from sharks, but they are closely related. They all have gill slits instead of gill covers and skeletons made of rubbery cartilage.

Which fish can shock?

The electric ray has special electric organs just behind its head. It gives off bursts of electricity to defend itself or to stun the fish it feeds on.

What has a sting on its tail?

Stingrays have poisonous spines on their whip-like tails. Some have one poisonous spine, others have several. They lie on the seabed with only their eyes and tail showing.

Stingray

Which eel becomes a fierce hunter?

When moray eels are young, they eat shrimps and tiny fish. But as they grow up, they learn to prey on larger and larger creatures.

Moray eel

Is it true?
Barracudas are attracted to jewelry.

Yes. In waters where barracudas are found, swimmers should take off any jewelry in case a passing barracuda takes a fancy to it!

Which tiny fish can strip an animal bare in minutes?

Piranhas live in rivers in South America where they hunt together in shoals of hundreds. With powerful jaws full of razor-sharp teeth, they may attack any large animal that enters the water.

Stonefish

? When is a stone not a stone?

When it's a stonefish. Stonefish are camouflaged so that it's almost impossible to see them amongst the rocks on the seabed. But sharp poisonous spines on their backs make them very dangerous to step on.

Piranha fish

Amazing! Many fish living in the cold, dark depths of the ocean look like monsters. They may have huge mouths full of sharp teeth, most are black and many can produce their own light.

Shark-proof bag

Amazing! In Australia in the 1930s, hundreds of sharks were caught in nets in just a few months. The numbers of many large sharks have gone down sharply all over the world because of hunting.

How can we prevent shark attacks?

Sharks have often attacked people who have survived shipwrecks or plane crashes far out at sea. Inflatable bags have been tested, which sharks tend to avoid. They can't detect moving limbs, electrical signals or blood inside them. Beaches can be protected by nets.

Great white shark

Is it true?
Nothing attacks a shark.

No. Sharks will attack each other. They are also attacked by whales, and even dolphins who will group together to protect their young. But the biggest threat of all comes from people.

Why do sharks attack?

When a shark attacks, it is often because it mistakes a swimmer or surfer for a seal or other prey. About 100 shark attacks are recorded on people each year. Many of the victims survive.

Who swims inside a cage?

Scientists studying dangerous sharks, such as the ocean white-tip and bull shark, often protect themselves inside a cage. The shark can bang the cage as much as it likes, but the diver is safe inside.

How can we learn more about sharks?

These days, people are more keen to learn about sharks. You can visit an aquarium to watch and find out more about these fascinating fish.

Amazing! Scientists can now tell a lot from some sharks' behavior. By studying a creature's movements and senses, they know when a shark is just being nosy, or when it's about to attack. By learning more, we may kill fewer sharks, and suffer fewer shark attacks.

Why do people kill sharks?

People kill millions of sharks every year, some to protect swimmers, others for food or just for sport. If too many are killed, sharks might disappear altogether.

Fisherman and catch

Which scientists dress like knights of old?

Scientists studying sharks sometimes wear chain-mail suits for protection. They may tag a shark's fins to learn how quickly and far it can travel.

Diver in chain-mail with blue shark

Is it true?
We've discovered all the sharks that exist.

No. Megamouth was first seen in 1976. Scientists think that there might be more sharks waiting to be discovered in the depths of the oceans.

Glossary

Air bladder An air-filled sac that helps keep fish afloat. Sharks do not have an air bladder, but have a huge oily liver instead.

Camouflage Colors, shape or markings of an animal that help it blend into its surroundings so that it is hard to see. The wobbegong shark has excellent camouflage.

Cartilage A rubbery, flexible material. The skeletons of sharks, rays and skate are made of cartilage.

Denticle The sharp points on a shark's skin.

Embryo A stage in development after an egg is fertilized until the young animal is born or hatches.

Fossil The preserved remains of something that was once alive.

Gills Breathing slits behind the head of a fish, used to extract oxygen from water.

Parasite A tiny animal that lives in or on another animal from which it gets its food. Parasites are often harmful to their "host".

Plankton Tiny animals and plants that float in the sea. Some of the larger sharks and several types of whales feed only on plankton which they filter from the water.

Predator An animal that hunts other animals for food.

Prey An animal that is hunted by another animal for food.

School A large number of the same kind of fish all swimming together. Hammerhead sharks swim in schools.

Index